Ireland's Best
TIN WHISTLE
TUNES FOR
CHILDREN

Waltons
PUBLISHING

NOTE

This book has been arranged in a manner that gradually introduces children to reading music on the stave. The beginners' section has the music on the stave with the names of the notes and the fingerings given under the stave. The intermediate section has the names of the *notes only* under the stave, and the subsequent sections are arranged according to tune types. Throughout the first two sections the learner is gradually introduced to the range of notes on the whistle, starting with just the three simplest notes for tune number one and expanding the range of notes used as the tunes progress. Within the first two sections, tunes have also been selected for the way they progress from simple rhythms and tempos to more difficult ones.

Simpler tunes of each type are given at the start of each of the sections of dance tunes. The author has included a number of his own tunes, specially composed to suit a particular stage of learning. These are numbers 11, 12, 21, 30, 43, 44, 58, 59, 68, 69, 76, 105 and 107.

For general notes on reading music and fingering charts, see:
- Key signatures, notes and fingering: page 4
- Note values: page 11
- Time signatures: page 39

The symbols ⌢ ⌣ over or under a note mean that the note may be held for as long as deemed appropriate.

Copyright © 2005 Walton Manufacturing Ltd.
Unit 6A, Rosemount Park Drive, Rosemount Business Park,
Ballycoolin Road, Dublin 11, Ireland

Compiled and Arranged • Harry Long
Setting • John Canning
Cover Design • Temple of Design

Book Alone: Order No. 1378
ISBN No. 1 85720 154 x

CD Edition: Order No. 1378cd
ISBN No. 1 85720 155 8

Exclusive Distributors:

Walton Manufacturing Co. Ltd.
Unit 6A, Rosemount Park Drive, Rosemount Business Park,
Ballycoolin Road, Dublin 11, Ireland

The James Import Company
9 Skyline Drive, Hawthorne, New York, NY 10532, USA

Printed in Ireland by Betaprint Ltd

1 3 5 7 9 0 8 6 4 2

CONTENTS

Key Signatures

Two main key signatures are used for tunes played on the 'D' tin whistle. One ♯ (sharp), which is F♯.

This is used for the key of G major and the key of E minor.

Two ♯s (sharps), which are F♯ and C♯.

This is used for the key of D major and the key of B minor.

The main difference between these key signatures for the whistle player is the way 'C' is played. (See fingering charts)

Scale of D – First (Lower) octave

● = Hole covered

○ = Hole uncovered

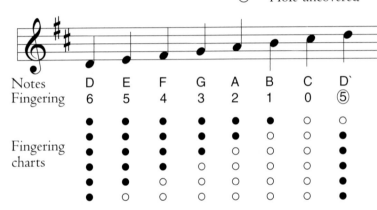

Notes	D	E	F	G	A	B	C	D`
Fingering	6	5	4	3	2	1	0	⑤

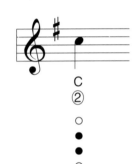

	C
	②

In the scale of G, the C is not sharp ♯, but natural and is played differently as shown here.

Scale of D – Second (higher) octave

Tunes 1 to 13 in this book do not go beyond the range of notes illustrated here. The tunes from 14 onward gradually introduce the learner to the higher notes.

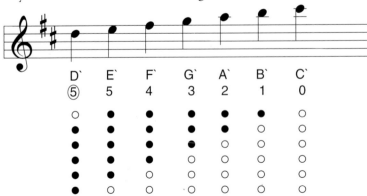

	D`	E`	F`	G`	A`	B`	C`
	⑤	5	4	3	2	1	0

Apart from D` (D high), all of the higher octave notes in the scale of D use the same fingering as the low octave notes. You simply blow harder for the higher notes. C natural in the high octave appears only rarely in tin whistle tunes and is not found in any of the tunes in this book.

The Mountains of Mourne (Air)

CHORD CHARTS FOR GUITAR

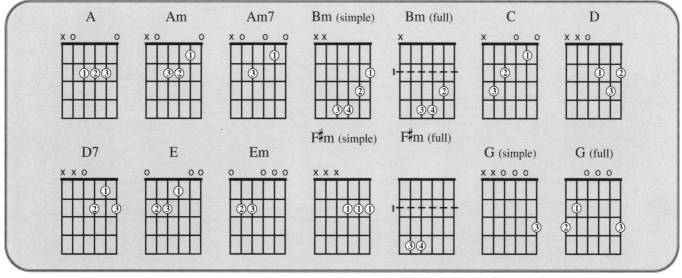

The Star of the County Down (Air)

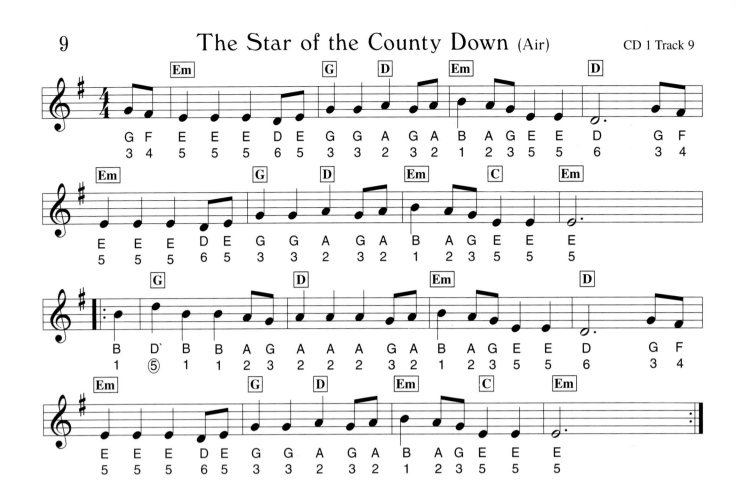

The Bog Down in the Valley-O (Polka)

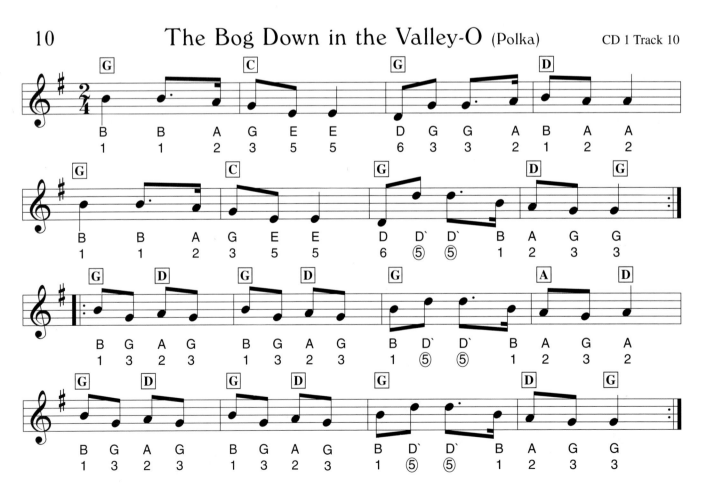

Arrangements copyright © 2005 Waltons Publications Ltd.

The Pooka Polka

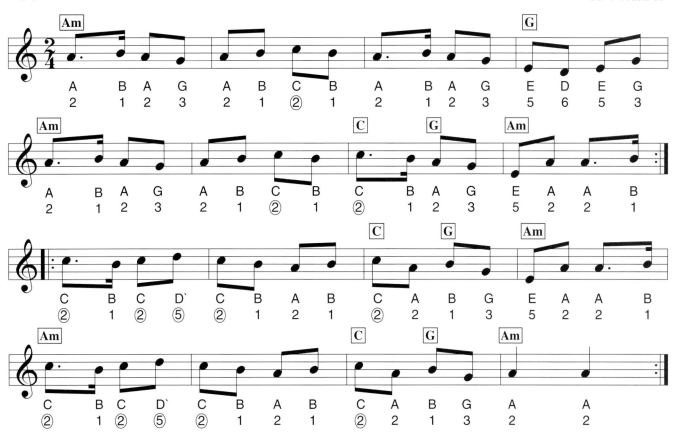

The Royal County March

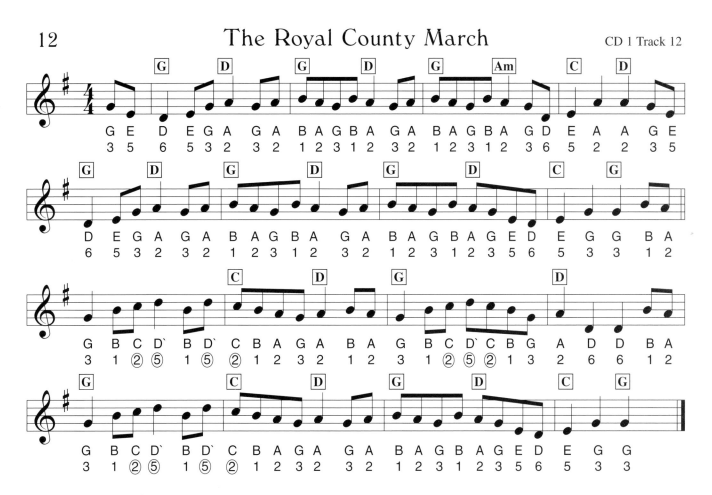

Lord of the Dance (Air)

My Singing Bird (Air)

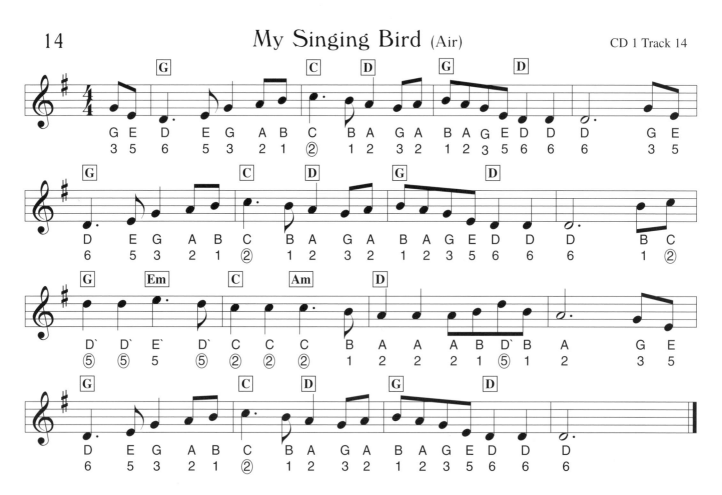

Raggle Taggle Gypsy (Air)

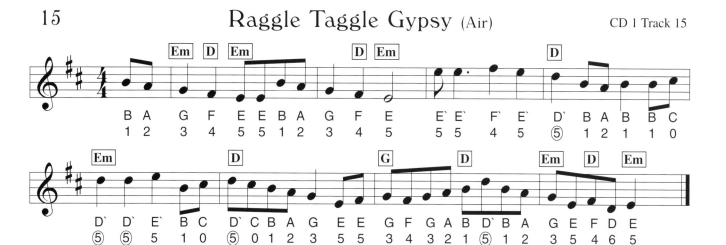

NOTE VALUES

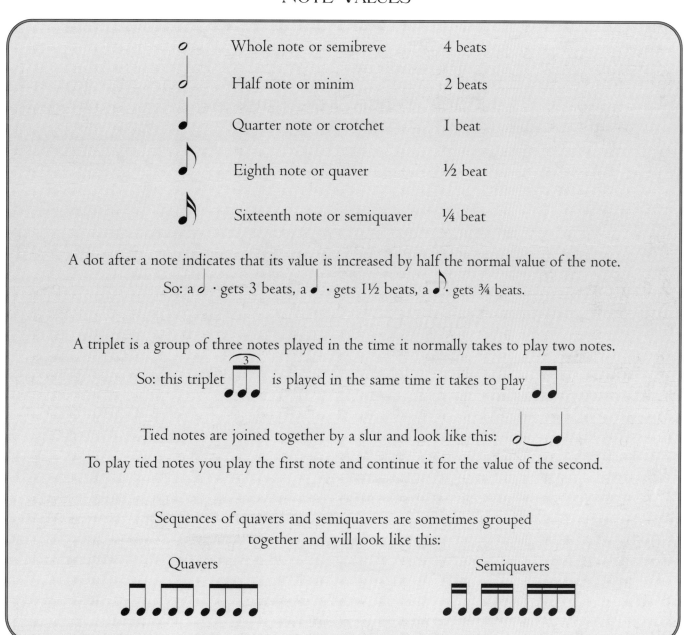

	Whole note or semibreve	4 beats
	Half note or minim	2 beats
	Quarter note or crotchet	1 beat
	Eighth note or quaver	½ beat
	Sixteenth note or semiquaver	¼ beat

A dot after a note indicates that its value is increased by half the normal value of the note. So: a 𝅗𝅥 · gets 3 beats, a ♩ · gets 1½ beats, a ♪ · gets ¾ beats.

A triplet is a group of three notes played in the time it normally takes to play two notes.

So: this triplet is played in the same time it takes to play

Tied notes are joined together by a slur and look like this:

To play tied notes you play the first note and continue it for the value of the second.

Sequences of quavers and semiquavers are sometimes grouped together and will look like this:

Quavers

Semiquavers

Daly's (Polka)

LOW WHISTLE (FEADÓG MHÓR)

Beidh Aonach Amárach (Air)

Arrangements copyright © 2005 Waltons Publications Ltd.

Emma's Farewell to Cortown (Air)

CD 1 Track 21

The Limerick Waltz

CD 1 Track 22

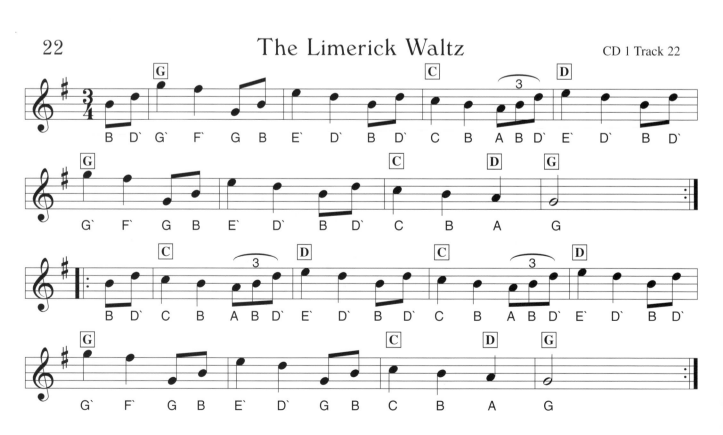

23 Father Halpin's Topcoat (Varsovienne)

24 Winter Is Past (Air)

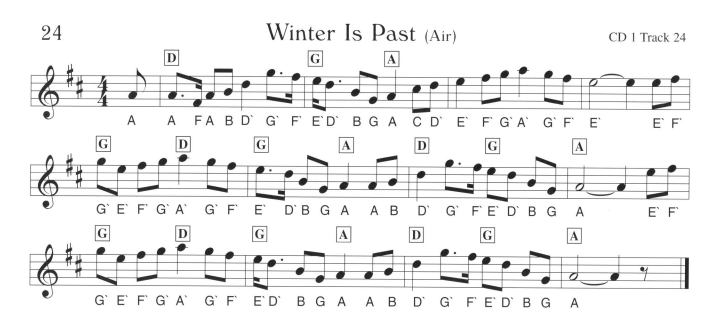

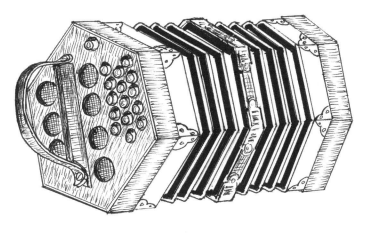

CONCERTINA (CONSAIRTÍN)

Arrangements copyright © 2005 Waltons Publications Ltd.

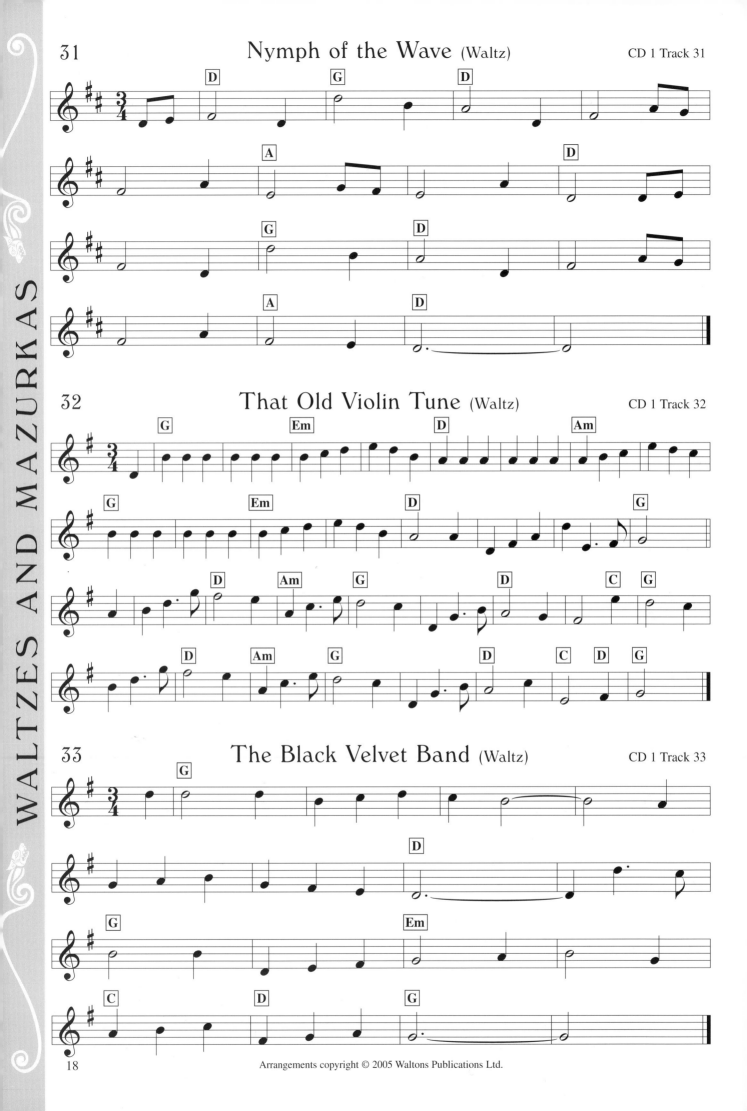

Nymph of the Wave (Waltz)

That Old Violin Tune (Waltz)

The Black Velvet Band (Waltz)

Sonny's Mazurka

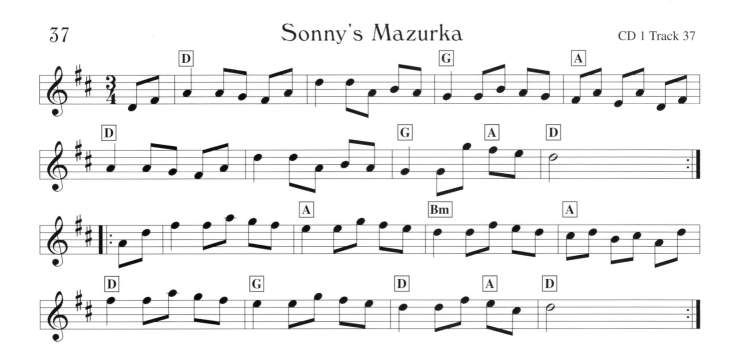

38 Johnny O'Leary's

39 Tá Dhá Ghabhairín Bhuí Agam

40 The Steamroller McTeige

POLKAS

Arrangements copyright © 2005 Waltons Publications Ltd.

The Road to Galway

The Magic Slipper

The Rathmore Polka

Pete's Polka

The Happy Polka

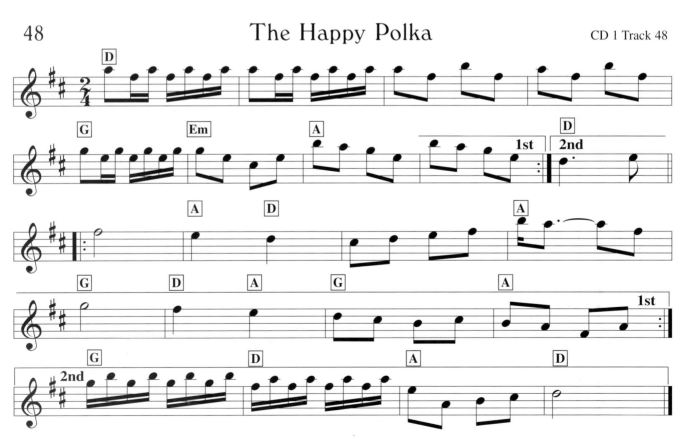

49   Hewlett   CD 1 Track 49

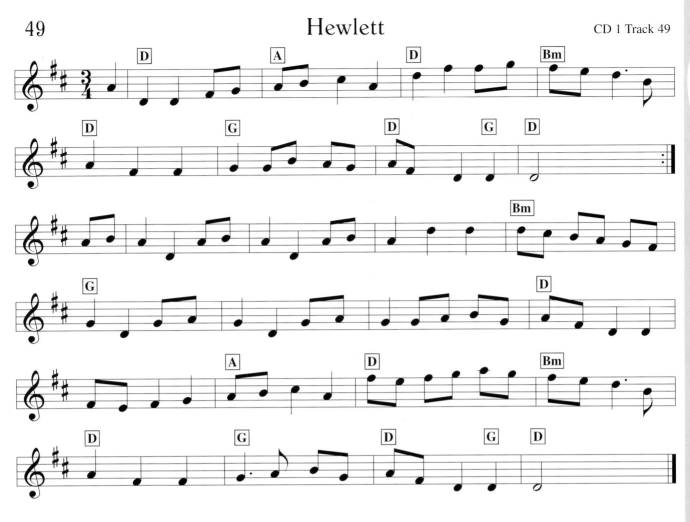

50   The Princess Royal   CD 1 Track 50

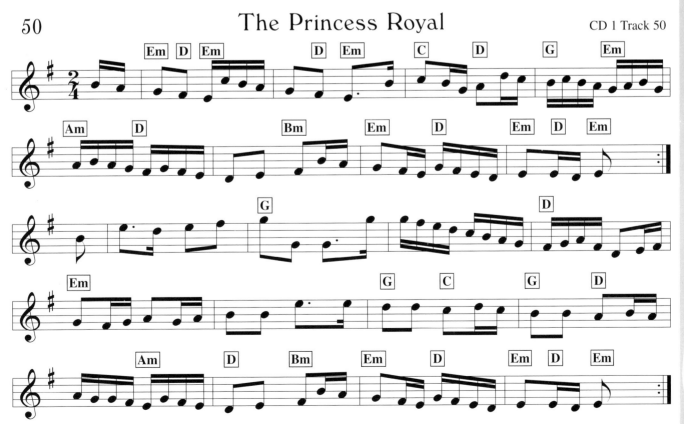

Miss Murphy

Bridget Cruise

WOODEN FLUTE (FLIÚT ADHMAID)

53   **Planxty Irwin**   CD 1 Track 53

54   **Sí Bheag Sí Mhór**   CD 1 Track 54

55   **Lady Gethin**   CD 1 Track 55

Carolan's Receipt

Planxty Burke

Arrangements copyright © 2005 Waltons Publications Ltd.

61 Nóra Chríonna   CD 2 Track 6

62 The Carraroe Jig   CD 2 Track 7

63 The Lilting Banshee   CD 2 Track 8

Pay the Reckoning

I Saw a Hawk in Dundalk

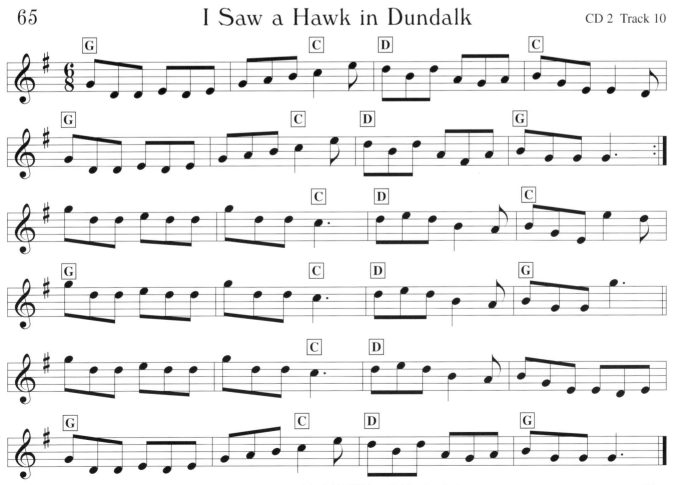

Arrangements copyright © 2005 Waltons Publications Ltd.

The Tara Jig

CD 2 Track 11

The Kesh Jig

CD 2 Track 12

MANDOLINE (MAINDILÍN)

68 **The Boys of Ballinlough** CD 2 Track 13

69 **The Ballinlough Lassies** CD 2 Track 14

70 **Bonaparte's March** CD 2 Track 15

Arrangements copyright © 2005 Waltons Publications Ltd.

Arrangements copyright © 2005 Waltons Publications Ltd.

The Wren's Hornpipe

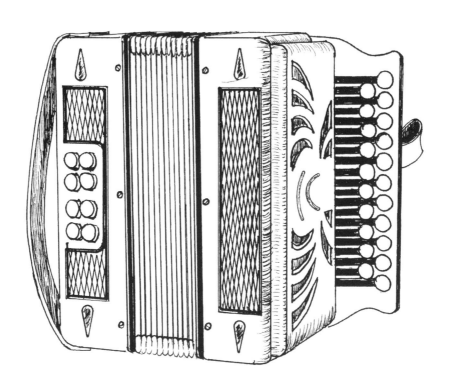

ACCORDION (CAIRDÍN – BOSCA CEOIL)

75 Dobbin's Flowery Vale

CD 2 Track 20

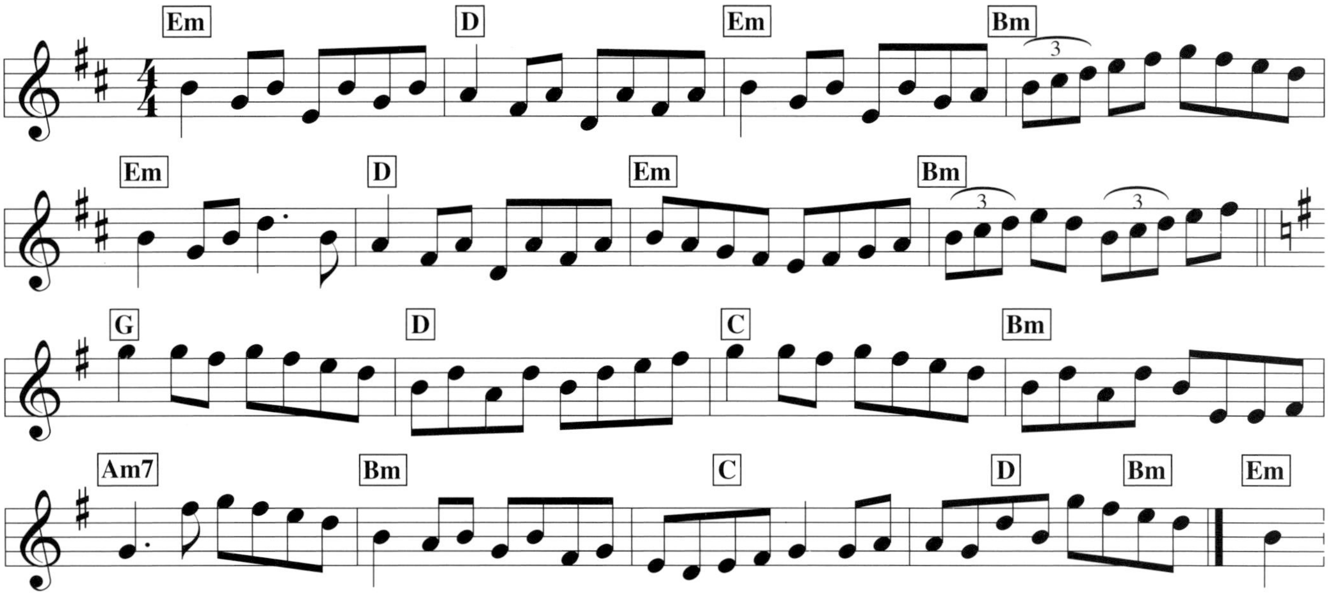

76 The Stackallen Reel

CD 2 Track 21

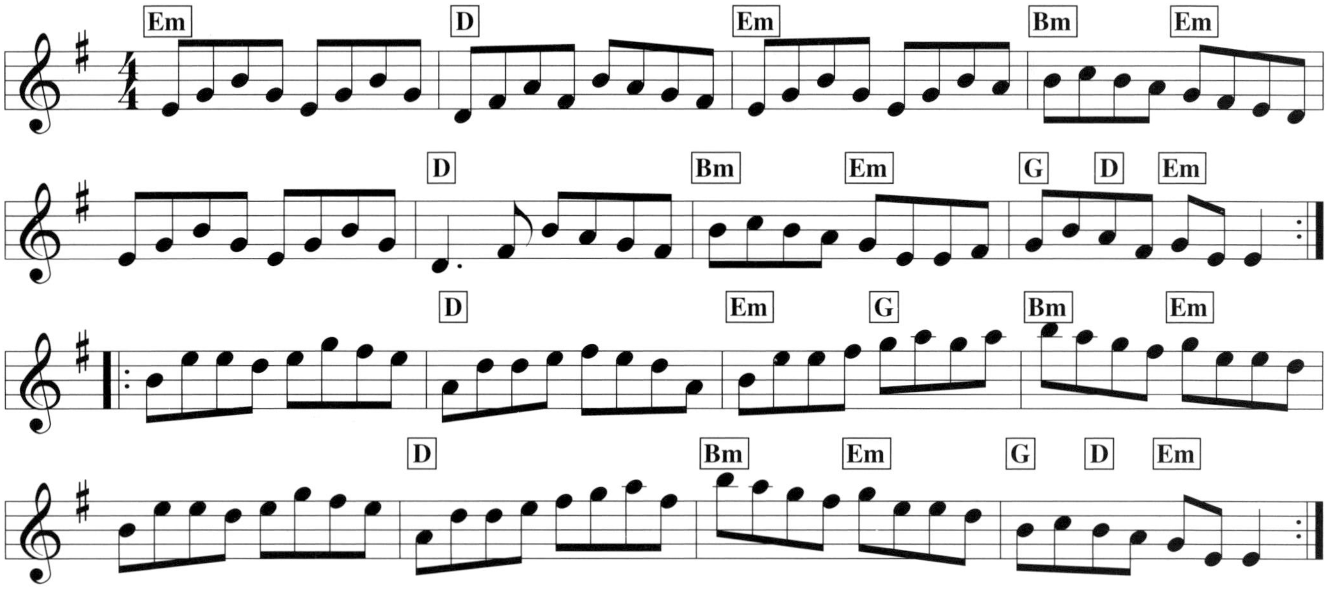

77 The Woman I Loved So Well

CD 2 Track 22

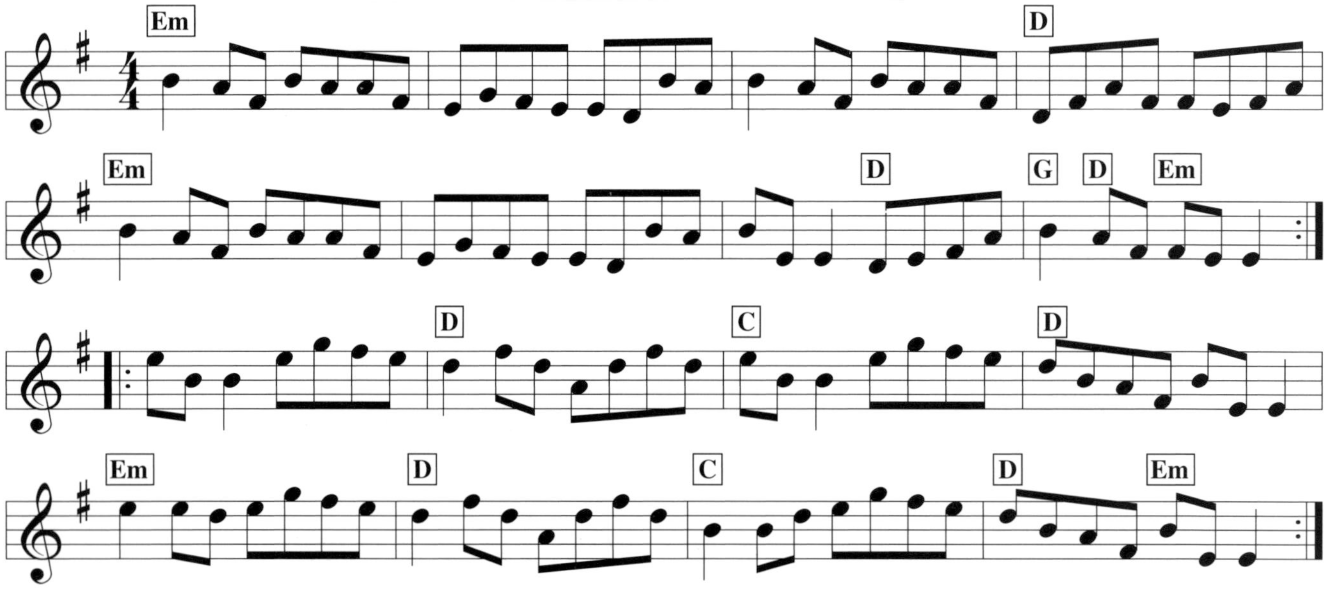

78 The Pullet CD 2 Track 23

79 The Milliner's Daughter CD 2 Track 24

80 Drowsy Maggie CD 2 Track 25

81 The Congress

82 The Glens of Aherlow

83 The Fisherman's Lilt

The Wise Maid

TIME SIGNATURES

The time signature appears at the start of each tune and consists of two numbers. The time signature for a common jig, for example, is: $\frac{6}{8}$

6 The top number indicates the number of beats in each bar.
8 The bottom number indicates the type of beat.

8 As the bottom number indicates quaver, or eighth beats.

4 As the bottom number indicates crotchet, or quarter beats.

FOLLOWING ARE THE DIFFERENT TIME SIGNATURES FOUND IN THIS BOOK:

$\frac{4}{4}$ 4 crotchet beats per bar. Found in marches, hornpipes and reels.

$\frac{3}{4}$ 3 crotchet beats per bar. Found in waltzes and mazurkas.

$\frac{2}{4}$ 2 crotchet beats per bar. Found in polkas.

$\frac{6}{8}$ 6 quaver beats per bar. Found in double jigs, also called common jigs or simply jigs.

$\frac{9}{8}$ 9 quaver beats per bar. Found in slip jigs.

$\frac{12}{8}$ 12 quaver beats per bar. Found in slides.

Nursery rhymes and song airs can use a number of different time signatures such as $\frac{3}{4}$ $\frac{2}{4}$ $\frac{4}{4}$ or $\frac{6}{8}$

85   **Jingle Bells**   CD 2 Track 30

86   **We Wish You a Merry Christmas**   CD 2 Track 31

87   **Away in a Manger**   CD 2 Track 32

88 **Silent Night** CD 2 Track 33

89 **Good King Wenceslas** CD 2 Track 34

90 **O Come All Ye Faithful** CD 2 Track 35

91 **Rug Muire Mac do Dhia** CD 2 Track 36

BANJO (BAINSEÓ)

98   The Lord's My Shepherd   CD 2 Track 43

99   Amazing Grace   CD 2 Track 44

100   Céad Míle Fáilte   CD 2 Track 45

101   Deus Meus Adiuva Me   CD 2 Track 46

102   A Íosa, Glan Mo Chroíse   CD 2 Track 47

An Spiorad Naomh Umainn

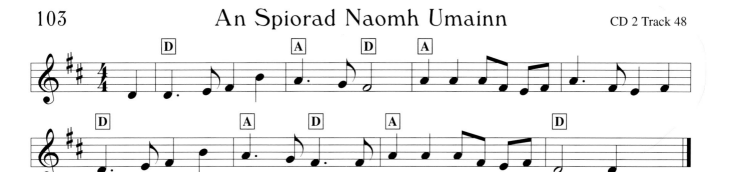

THE BRIAN BORU HARP (CRUIT – CLÁIRSEACH)

104 The Scattery Island Slide

CD 2 Track 49

105 The Harmony March

CD 2 Track 50

Lento = Slow; Moderato = At a moderate speed; Accelerando = Getting gradually faster

106 The First Slip (Slip Jig)

CD 2 Track 51

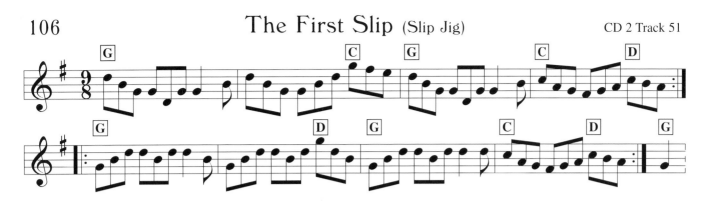

107 The Kilbeg Air

CD 2 Track 52

108 Going to the Well for Water (Slide)

CD 2 Track 53

Arrangements copyright © 2005 Waltons Publications Ltd.

O Love of the North (Air)

CD 2 Track 54

110

Amhrán na bhFiann (Irish National Anthem)

CD 2 Track 55

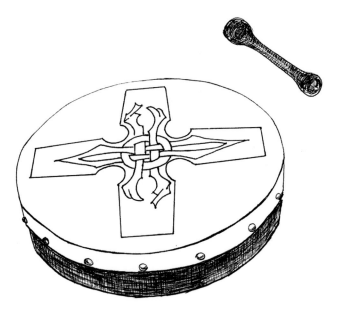

BODHRÁN